Table of Contents

Dedication
Foreword
Introduction
Chapter 1: The Day of Atonement
Chapter 2: The Sabbath Years
Chapter 3: Return To Your Home
Chapter 4: Living Within Your Means
Chapter 5: Valuing Others
Chapter 6: Trust God's Process
Chapter 7: It Is Only Temporary
Chapter 8: Reclaim Your Family
Chapter 9: Return The Property
Chapter 10: Help Others
Chapter 11: RELEASE!
Conclusion

Dedication

I dedicate this book to my family, blood and not, because of their tireless support and encouragement for everything that I do. We may fuss and fight, but when it counts you all are always here for me. I couldn't choose just one person because you all have helped in one way or another.

Foreword

I started my career as a professional football journalist covering the Washington Redskins. After spending five years as a credentialed media member, the Lord began to stir a deeper passion in my heart for worship and ministry. I now work as the Worship Director at Avert Church and am a Christian artist.

Many are the plans in our heart, but the Lord's purpose will always prevail. We may not always know where the Lord is leading us, but Him leading us is paramount. Our duty is to live surrendered lives unto Christ. Always willing and always available.

One of the ministries I have the privilege of co-leading is for young adults. James started attending our young adult bible studies and gatherings nearly a year ago. It was clear upon my initial interaction with James that he is truly a man of God.

He is mature in his walk with Jesus. He has wisdom beyond his years. It is also very apparent that his love for the Lord has truly fueled his love for others. James cares about people and he cares about ministry. Truly he is a willing vessel who has made himself completely available to the Lord. It's no surprise that "The Year of Jubilee" will become the first of I'm certain many books that James authors.

Not only does this book give a clear exegesis of an Old Testament text, but it also gives practical application to our current everyday lives. The Old Testament can be difficult to comprehend. Many struggle to find parallels from the Old Testament to modern times. Arguably none more challenging than the book of Leviticus. Yet, James finds a thread that is true throughout scripture - Jesus.

"The Year of Jubilee" begins with a comprehensive reminder that Jesus saves. "Christ paid for our sins once and for all on the cross," James writes in chapter 1. Making this point at the beginning of the book is important contextually because it immediately offers the gospel to all readers. Looking at the Old Testament through the lens of the Gospel helps bring clarity and depth to our theology.

I have witnessed James' vast understanding of scripture in our young adult small group. His input during the discussion on scripture has helped shift and challenge perspectives. He is a valued voice among the members of our small group.

As a leader, it's always great to know you can truly depend on others. James has been consistent. When he speaks, I'm always certain that his opinions are both thoughtful and wise.

Whether it's in worship leading or teaching, I am a strong believer in scriptural accuracy. All of scripture is God-breathed and applicable to our lives. I am glad that James has taken this lesser discussed topic and highlighted its gospel parallels. As he eloquently explains, "The Year of Jubilee" is one that can be experienced in your life right now.

Giving all glory and honor to Jesus,

Manny Benton
Artist, Worship Director at Avert Church

Introduction

The process of publishing this book began during the Covid-19 pandemic of 2020 that shook the world to its knees. This was a time in history where a virus made millions around the world sick, claimed thousands of lives, shut down countries, and shut people in their homes. While many people were asked to stay in their homes, only essential personnel were allowed to continue to work as we worked together to stop the spread of this virus. While some may think that CEOs, business owners, and other high profile positions were essential to the functioning of our world, this pandemic revealed to us the real essential personnel workers.

These essential workers were custodial workers, teachers, nurses, garbage collectors, truck drivers, mail carriers, farmers, and grocery store employees. These are just a few of the many important jobs that are irreplaceable. However, many of these essential workers were looked at as menial and often taken advantage of prior to this event. While nobody would openly say these people were not important, it was shown by their minimum wage pay and benefits, lack of respect by others, and marginalization as many people took them for granted. This pandemic should teach everyone to rethink, repent, and refocus on the truly important things and important people around us.

Now what does that have to do with the topic of this book (I know you thought that). God has given us many commands and principles in the Bible. Commands to obey Him, love our neighbor, and treat others with respect. Many commands that the children of

Israel followed to keep themselves in line with God until Jesus came to set us free from the law and sin. This book will discuss a lesser-known command in the Old Testament, but a command that could have made the Israelites the most prosperous people of all time. The command discussed in this book shows how we can shift our priorities to create more freedoms for more people. The Year of Jubilee is discussed in the book of Leviticus, the third book of the Holy Bible, chapter 25. I advise you to read and study this chapter for yourself and research this event for more understanding. "Wisdom is the principal thing; therefore get wisdom: and with all thy getting get understanding" **(Proverbs 4:7)**

    This book breaks down each aspect of the Year of Jubilee as well as how each aspect relates to our world today. Please take your time in reading this book, so that you can gain the full essence of the Year of Jubilee and how it can radically change our world for a stronger future. I pray that everyone who reads this book will receive it well and learn some ways to improve your personal life. In Jesus Name, Amen.

Chapter 1: Day of Atonement

"The beginning of atonement is the sense of its necessity"
- Lord George Gordon Byron

The History

The Year of Jubilee is ushered in through the Day of Atonement. Leviticus 16 explains the Old Testament rituals associated with the Day of Atonement. In short, the High Priest sacrificed a goat to God in order to atone for the sins of the people. Then, he put the sins of the people on another goat, called the scapegoat, and sent it into the wilderness. This process would cover the people's sins by the blood, and remove their sins from them by sending the scapegoat into the wilderness. The death of these two animals told God that the people obeyed His commands for the forgiveness of sin. This was the Old Testament process of forgiving sins. However, God has given us a new way.

The New Covenant way is through the life, works, death, and resurrection of Jesus Christ, our Lord and Savior. We no longer have to sacrifice goats and lambs to God to atone for our sins. Christ paid for our sins ONCE and for ALL on the cross. To bring atonement for our sins, all we need to do is accept and declare verbally that Jesus Christ as Lord, and believe in our hearts that God raised Him from the dead **(Romans 10:9)**. Once we have taken that step, our sins have been cleansed and forgiven by the blood of Jesus. Since Christ paid for it all, any day can be a day of atonement. We must repent of our sins toward God and He is faithful and righteous to forgive us of those sins and cleanse us from all unrighteousness **(1 John 1:9)**.

How It Can Apply Today

On the Day of Atonement, all of God's people got together to confess their sins to the high priest (Jesus is now the High Priest).

This communal confession allowed everyone to get the negative thoughts and actions off their chest while releasing the control those thoughts and actions had over the people. This command can improve both our natural lives and spiritual lives. Communal confession can allow people who think they are different to express common experiences. Those who think they are better than others will slowly become humble as they hear similar sins. Those who feel inferior will find peace. Those who feel alone will find support and encouragement. This command can be used to bring an end to judgment, discrimination of all types, depression, anger, and other negative feelings associated with sin. This is not a cure for any mental health issues, but it can be used as a coping mechanism and recovery technique in therapy.

    In the spiritual, the Day of "True" Atonement (Jesus' crucifixion) brought the final cleansing by which people and the land could be forgiven. This spiritual day of atonement released us from the ritual repetition of animal sacrifices by giving us an eternal sacrifice that covers all sin for all time. The only sacrifice we have to make is sacrificing our earthly lives for a better heavenly life with God through Jesus. This day of atonement can be a different day for each person, but the acts are still the same. We confess our sins to the High Priest (Jesus). He took ALL of our sins and died as the perfect sacrifice for our sins. We are now cleansed from these sins because of the redemptive work of Christ on the cross and by our confession **(Revelation 12:11)**. Jesus can atone for your sins any day as long as you confess and seek forgiveness.

Tips On What You Can Do Now

There are plenty of easy ways in which you can implement the principles of the Day of Atonement for your everyday life.
- Spiritually: To accept Jesus Christ as your personal Lord and Savior, you simply need to:
    - Acknowledge that we are all sinners in need of a Savior, which means that we have all done things that have separated us from God **(Romans 3:23)**
    - Believe in your heart that He died for your sins and that God raised Him from the dead, which brings you into a new life for FREE. **(Romans 10:9)**
    - Confess with your mouth that Jesus is your Lord and Savior, which means you accept His love, grace, leadership, and guidance **(Romans 10:9)**
- Mentally/Emotionally: Use this day to begin the process of healing from unforgiveness. Hold a conversation that will allow all parties involved to share their experiences related to the offense. Once similar feelings and experiences are brought to light, it will be easier to start the building of trust. **Warning:** This step will be difficult. But remember, forgiveness is mainly for you and not the other person. Forgiveness will take time and you may need to repeatedly forgive them in your heart. If you really want to pursue your healing, then it takes a conscious effort day by day or moment by moment **(Matthew 18:21-22)**. Walking in forgiveness will purge your heart and spirit of negativity which will free you to walk in the love of Jesus Christ.

Discussion

- In your life, who do you think needs to apologize to you?
- Who do you need to apologize to?
- Will you forgive even if the other person does not apologize?

Chapter 2: The Sabbath Years

[Handwritten calendar for May 2020 showing trash days on the 6th, 13th, 20th, and 27th; "Rest" circled on the 10th; basketball games noted on the 2nd, 9th, 16th, and 30th; "Play offs" on the 23rd.]

"Sabbath isn't about resting perfectly; it's about resting in the One who is perfect."
- Shelly Miller

The History

The Sabbath Years are important preparation for the Year of Jubilee. Every seventh year was to be a restful year for the land. This period of rest gives the land time to refresh and replenish its nutrients to prepare for the planting of the following year. The Sabbath Year is important for the people as well. This period without planting and harvesting gave people time to refocus on other important things, such as spending intimate time with God, building relationships, or tending to their homes. This tradition would have made the land and the people more prosperous in the following year. The Year of Jubilee is the seventh Sabbath Year (every 50 years). Seven is a biblical number for completion with examples of the number of days God took to create AND rest on the seventh day.

How It Can Apply Today

Today, we can use this tradition exactly as is or adjust it for the sake of time. If a city, state, or nation were to follow this Sabbath Year tradition, there would be many benefits. The region would place their faith in God to provide enough resources to sustain the people and property until the harvest of the eighth year. The region would live within their means during the Sabbath Year. This would: reduce debt accrued from overspending, increase frugal spending, and improve local economies. The overspending debts would decrease because the area is only spending what is necessary. Communities would begin to shop smarter by buying in bulk or finding other ways to reduce costs, such as recycling or zero-waste lifestyles. Local spending, which reduces shipping costs, would grow the economy by investing within the system and not outsourcing it to other territories.

On a personal level, people would have fewer debts over time from overspending as well. This extra time and resources could be spent with God, family, friends, in community service, or simply saving extra resources that are not necessarily needed. This saving will increase energy levels, improve income, as well as teach humility, gratitude, and appreciation of resources. This process could take the full year or shorter depending on the size of the goal. One could start small by taking a week of Sabbath rest to live within their means by watching how they spend and gradually work their way up to the full year.

    This process of Sabbath rest must be repeated! The repetition is stated by God in Leviticus 25. This repetition builds consistency, shows dedication, and improves obedience to God. Repetition can also indicate that the repeated task is very important. This Sabbath rest should be observed outside of the Sabbath Years at the end of the week as commanded in the 10 Commandments **(Exodus 20:8-11)**. By taking this rest period, you show God that you are committed to taking time out for you to gain a closer and stronger relationship with Him. This rest is to be observed by EVERYONE in your household. Anyone attached to you, including family and employees, should be allowed to rest while you are resting. This will give them time to spend on more important things, such as time with God, as well as refresh their energy. This set time of refreshment will increase morale, productivity, and efficiency.

    In the spiritual, this Sabbath rest is probably the most important step toward your Jubilee. Setting aside personal time with Jesus, away from the hassle and headaches of daily life, does wonders. Spend this time reading the Bible, praying, fasting, worshiping the LORD, and singing Gospel music. Join with fellow believers and testify about how God has worked in your life. Joining together as the Body of Christ is more important now than ever **(Hebrews 10:24-25)**. This Sabbath rest helps refresh the soul and brings a closer walk with the Father. A closer walk with the Father will guide us through God's will. A closer walk will bring clarity of purpose, reduce anxiety, and increase happiness. More time with Jesus means more peace that passes understanding. **(Philippians 4:7)**.

Tips On What You Can Do Now

- Budget to save one month's paycheck each year. After accounting for your necessary expenses, you can save one month's paycheck each year and not spend it (except for emergencies)
- One day each week, only perform essential tasks and seek to avoid any work-related issues or concerns. Take a two week period during the year to focus on relaxation, refocus, and preparation. DO NOT avoid responsibilities needed for daily living.

Discussion

- How will you spend your Sabbath rest with God?
- How will you spend your Sabbath rest with family or loved ones?
- How will you prepare yourself and your household to thrive during the Sabbath rest?

Chapter 3: Return To Your Home

"There's no place like home." - Dorothy Gale

The History

A unique aspect of the Year of Jubilee was that everyone returned to their homeland or home property. This home refers to your place of origin, the place where you grew up, the place of your family. In the Old Testament, the Hebrew people lived over a vast area because God had blessed them with so much land. There would be cities and villages where people would own property. If one wanted an additional property, other than your home, one would purchase it, much like today. The land was distributed by God for all of the 12 tribes of Israel. Each tribe had their portion, except for the tribe of Levi which was given the tabernacle as their portion. Children and families would leave home and go about their lives (start new families, buy new property, etc.). The Jubilee would have people return to their home territory according to their clan or tribe.

How It Can Apply Today

With the busy hustle and bustle of today's society, people can lose track of the importance of family and family time. Family is not always the blood relatives, but the people you love and truly care for and who care about you **(Mark 3:35)**. The Year of Jubilee gives people that opportunity to reconnect with family, their hometown, and old friends that they have not seen in a while. This visit can help put life back into perspective. A healthy perspective of God and family first will lead to better decision-making, productivity, and rejuvenation. There are many stories of people who were feeling stressed, tired, and unmotivated because of the busyness of life. Such a person would then return home for a family gathering or just to get away from the stress. This person would relax at home with family, reconnect with friends, and reminisce about old times during adolescence. This time at home refreshed the person and their outlook on life changed for the better. Do you need to be rejuvenated?

      In the spiritual, returning home means returning to God. We are just passing through this life on our way back to God. The Year of Jubilee is our time to truly return to God. Life has a way of getting in the way of our relationship with God. We become distracted by jobs, worries, money, and other earthly things that will fade away. God wants us to return our focus to Him in order to strengthen our relationship and loosen our dependency on the world. We can return home spiritually by going back to church (the Body of Christ, not just the building). Spend time in prayer together, share testimonies about what God is doing, and sing praises together to Jesus for whatever you've been dealing with, good AND bad. This time will refresh your soul to be ready to face life with a new perspective. The Holy Spirit will come to give us the power to be witnesses and rejoice in the Name of the LORD **(Acts 1:8)**. We are still human. We will make mistakes in life. This is often a problem for many in the body of Christ. We make a mistake and then put all this shame and disappointment on ourselves. This process repeats and develops into spiritual depression and anxiety. When these thoughts or anxieties start, read **Romans 8:1**: Therefore, there is now no condemnation for those in Christ Jesus. Jesus already paid it all, so tell him all about it and He will cleanse us of all unrighteousness **(1 John 1:9)**.

Tips On What You Can Do Now

Returning home physically, mentally, economically, and spiritually can greatly benefit you and the community around you. Here are some ways you can return home during your Year of Jubilee:

- Physically: Go visit some friends and family you have not seen in a while. Our hustle in life can sometimes get in the way of spending quality time with those who love and care for us.
    - If forgiveness needs to be done before you can go back, refer to the "Tips On What You Can Do Now" section of chapter 1. If your past family and friends are not beneficial to your current growth and progress, be careful to guard your heart while visiting. Your presence can encourage them to grow and mature, however, being around them could hinder your current progress. Guard your heart above all else because it is the source of life **(Proverbs 4:23)**
    - Another way to return home physically is to volunteer within your community or the community you came from. Volunteer through local churches, schools, food banks, and any other community service-related organizations. This is beneficial to you and the community.
- Mentally: Returning home mentally can help us remain humble and focused on our progress. Remember the things you used to do, places you used to go, and thoughts you used to think. Remembering where God has brought you from

will build humility, gratitude, and enable us to extend grace toward others.
- Economically: Returning home economically can look like supporting local businesses within your community. This helps to build local economies, which will help support community improvements.

Discussion

- What are some things you are glad you no longer do?
- How can you guard your heart while remembering where God has brought you from?
- How has returning home inspired you to help others?

Chapter 4: Living Within Your Means

RENT	$300.00
FOOD	$200.00
TRAVEL	$100.00
SAVING	$500.00
ENTERTAINMENT	$50.00

"Do not save what is left after spending, but spend what is left after saving."

— Warren Buffett

The History

During the Year of Jubilee, as in Sabbath Years, the people were not allowed to plant or harvest their fields. God promised to supply enough food from the previous harvest to last until the harvest of the year after the Sabbath year. The Year of Jubilee follows a Sabbath year, so the people had to survive from three years on the harvest from one year (if that is not a blessing, I don't know what it is). Since the people could not plant or harvest, they had to manage what they used from the harvests to make sure God's blessing lasted until they harvested again. God will supply all our needs **(Philippians 4:19)**, but we must make sure we do not become greedy or gluttonous and over-consume what we are given.

How It Can Apply Today

Living within our means is a difficult concept for us today, especially those in first world countries. We live in a time where everyone has a credit card and is not afraid to use it. Even the highest governments in the land cannot seem to live within their means. At the time of this writing, the United States currently has almost $21.2 trillion dollars worth of debt. Now the average American doesn't have nearly that much debt, but with student loans, car loans, housing markets, and the ever-increasing "need to have it all", people are accruing more and more debt each year. It's time to start a year of Jubilee and live within our means. Start by tearing up the credit cards! If you can't afford it, you don't need it. Except in the case of emergencies, never use your credit card. The temptation to buy will be there, but God will lead you away from that desire through discipline.

Next, set a budget and stick to it. Take your annual income, set aside your tithes (because God deserves His firstfruits Leviticus 23), and calculate your bills, emergencies, and other expenses. If you cannot live within those means, try to eliminate some of the unnecessary expenses, like eating out, extra jewelry, new clothes just because, etc. Try to use coupons, savings deals, and cheaper substitutes as much as possible. If you think you can live comfortably, then start paying off some debts that you have with any surplus money. Living within your means is tough, but preparing for it makes it easier to accomplish. Remember: God will always provide your needs (not always your wants).

In the spiritual, living within your means might be an even harder task. We tend to put others first, say 'yes' to just about anything people ask, and forget about ourselves. This is a type of spiritual debt that we have put on ourselves. Even though Jesus paid it all **(John 3:16),** some Christians put new burdens on ourselves without a break. We are still human, and that means we need time to rest.

I know two people very well that push themselves to their limits and beyond sometimes with everything they do. They work long hours and then come home to church events that they need to attend. They rarely have a weekend off because of different church events. They are often exhausted from the weekend that they did not gain the necessary rest to begin the workweek. These two people are truly dedicated to the LORD and the body of Christ, but it's time to live within our limits. It is okay to say no to some events for rest and refreshing purposes. Unless the event cannot happen without your presence, you have the choice to go or rest. Pray about your decision because God knows you better than you know yourself and will never steer you wrong.

Tips On What You Can Do Now

Living within your means is incredibly important as God has called us to be lenders and not borrowers. Discipline and grace are important during this time. Saving money is often hard as temptation and FOMO (fear of missing out) are trying to influence us to spend. As you grow during this time, extend grace to yourself if you slip up and overspend, BUT remember the purpose behind you living within your means. Here are some simple tips to start living within your means:

- Limit the amount of times you use your credit card(s). Strive to use your card(s) only ONCE this year in order to keep the card active and not lowering your credit score. Buy something of small value and pay it off immediately.
- Use any extra money you have saved from the "Sabbath Years" to help pay off debts. This will help you to not spend this money on frivolous things.
- Do a Needs Assessment of what things are considered needs and what things are considered wants. Define what needs and wants are for your specific living situation.

- <u>Avoid comparison</u> to others by focusing on your household and your responsibilities.

Discussion

- Are there any unnecessary subscriptions/memberships you can cancel?
- What tools can you use to add more time and less stress?
- What plans can you cancel to manage your time better?

Chapter 5: Don't Take Advantage

"Never look down on anyone unless you're helping them up"
- Jesse Jackson

The History

Leviticus 25:14-17 describes how to buy and sell during the Year of Jubilee. The Israelites were to buy and/or sell amongst their own people. The price of purchasing was to be set based on the number of years since the Jubilee. The price of selling was to be set based on the number of years left for harvesting. Basically, their stock market was set on timing and necessity. If the number of years was plentiful, the price would increase because there was still time to use the land before returning it in the Jubilee (v. 16a). If the number of years was short, then the price would decrease because the recipient would have less time to utilize the land before returning it (v. 16b). How does this compare to buying and selling of today?

How It Can Apply Today

The basic rule of economics is supply and demand. This principle states that when the supply is low with a high demand, the price must increase. When the supply is high with a low demand, the price must decrease. This is designed to maximize the profit for a business. This is seen in many fields from medicine to hospitality to criminal justice. If the demand for a limited number of hotel rooms is high, the price goes up so that the hotel can maximize revenue. If the demand for rooms is low, the price goes down so that they can at least make some money. In the long run, the highs and lows even out. However, some fields are taking advantage of people when it comes to this principle. The Word tells us to flip this concept around when it comes to buying and selling. The land was to be sold in the opposite way. If a person had more time to use the product, then the price should increase. If a person had less time to use the product, then the price should decrease. For example, if a doctor has a patient that is in desperate need of some medicine or operation, the price of said procedure would be extremely costly. The opposite occurs for something milder. Those in need who are desperate should not have to pay an arm and a leg to get their arm or leg fixed. Using this principle, those in need would be able to get what they need much easier. If individuals, groups, cities, even nations would utilize supply and demand in this fashion, there would be fewer people in debt, poverty, and subpar living conditions. With fewer people in debt, they could use their extra money for other things thus keeping the flow of money strong within the system. This concept seems ridiculous to some, but since we are one large community under God, we must show reverence for the LORD by not taking advantage of others in their time of need **(Leviticus 25:17)**. This goes for any manner of taking advantage, not just financially. Bottom line: DO NOT TAKE ADVANTAGE OF EACH OTHER!

  In the spiritual, taking advantage of others happens more than one might think. We can take advantage of someone's generosity by consistently asking for something knowing they won't refuse. We take silence as agreement when it comes to the person who doesn't speak up for themselves. We even take advantage of God's grace when we choose to sin, "repent", repeat. We all have our temptations that affect us more than other ones. We sin, we ask for forgiveness and say we won't do it again, and we end up choosing to commit the same sin again. God's grace is sufficient **(2 Corinth 12:9)** and renewed daily **(Lamentations 3:23)**, but we cannot purposely commit sin because we know God will forgive us

(Hebrew 10:26). God's grace is only sufficient when we choose to accept it to change our ways and turn from the sin **(Romans 6:15)**. If we purposely choose sin over what is right on a consistent basis, we are not true followers of Christ. Don't take advantage of God's grace. You won't lose your salvation, but you won't see God move as much as you could.

Tips On What You Can Do Now

Since this concept is about making sure that everyone has what they need based on what is theirs, not taking advantage of others means to respect anything you borrow from or give to others **(Matthew 18:23-35)**.

- If you lend something, do so with grace in your heart. If the person needs to continue to use what you've lent them beyond the Year of Jubilee, extend grace. Make sure that they are using your property properly and not abusing it. However, do not add on more "repayment" or stipulations on top of the original agreement. Once you have inspected your property, return it to them until they finish their need for it.
- If you borrow something, do so with wisdom in your heart. If it is close to the year of Jubilee, use wisdom. Determine if the need is really necessary and can be done within the time before the property must be returned. Do not allow the other person to take advantage of you. Also, do not take advantage of anyone's generosity. Remember: this concept is meant to strengthen the community.

Discussion

- Do you have any unreasonable expectations for yourself and others?
- How can you participate in social justice activities?
- How can you participate in community service activities?

Chapter 6: Trust God's Process

"Trusting God's plan is the only secret I know in the gentle art of not freaking out."
- Lysa TerKeurst

The History

Leviticus 25:18-22 is the most important part of the Year of Jubilee. These verses teach us that if we follow God's commands and trust Him to deliver, then we will live safely in our land and have what we need to survive and then some. The Israelites were prone to complaining about what God was doing. When the Israelites left Egypt, they complained about how it would have been better to serve the Egyptians than to die in the wilderness **(Exodus 14:10-12)**. They wanted to be free of the slavery in Egypt, but when God was in the process of bringing them out, they got worried. They forgot that God said He would save them or they didn't trust Him because of what they were seeing. With the Year of Jubilee, the Israelites would have to go without farming the land for two-plus years! Now that's a long time to go without knowing how you will eat. However, God promised them that if they followed His commands, that He would bless the harvest before the Sabbath year with food enough to last until they harvested again in the year after the Jubilee. They must live by faith, not sight, and trust God's process. We must do the same **(2 Corinthians 5:7)**.

How It Can Apply Today

Today, we all face similar times of not trusting God. Be honest! I know I have been a little worried about money when I started going to university. I was concerned about how to pay for it, where to live, what kind of job I would need to sustain all those bills and still eat. Thank God I have Him who controls the universe. I prayed and put the situations in His hands, and I am still feeling the blessings that followed. God is the God of abundance. Jesus said *I have come so that they may have life and have it in abundance* **(John 10:10).** Putting your trust in God to deliver on His promises is a hard task, especially for us humans. However, trusting God to deliver has amazing benefits. The more we trust God with our lives, the less worry we have about the unknown. The more we follow God's commands, the less decisions we have to make (come on, y'all are indecisive just like me). This reduced worry, stress, and indecisiveness will improve overall productivity and increase time to handle priorities such as spending time with God and family.

In the spiritual, we face many demons and evil spirits that want to steal our joy and well-being. The demons of anxiety and fear have a strong grip on the body of Christ. Even though we serve an almighty God, we still find ourselves worrying about what others think, how good we are or aren't, and where God is taking us. Hebrews 11 is a key chapter for faith. These heroes of faith will show you how to improve your faith through their stories of God's triumph. God knows us, where we're going, and how we're going to get there. Practice trust falling into God's hands little by little to develop your faith muscles. Slowly, you'll start trusting God to deliver even when there appears to be nothing in sight. As Solomon wrote in Proverbs 3:5-6, *Trust in the Lord with all your heart, and lean not to your own understanding. In your ways acknowledge Him, and He will direct your paths.*

Tips On What You Can Do Now

During this trust process, remind yourself of God's promises daily. When you need a reminder of why you're doing this or where

your resources will come from, here are some of God's promises that can help you:
- The LORD will fight for you; you need only to be still (Exodus 14:14)
- But those who wait on the LORD will renew their strength. They will soar on wings like eagles, will run and not get weary, will walk and not faith (Isaiah 40:31)
- For I know the plans I have for you, declares the LORD, plans to prosper you and not to harm you. To give you a hope and a future (Jeremiah 29:11)
- "But seek first his kingdom and his righteousness, and all these things will be given to you as well." (Matthew 6:33)
- "Jesus looked at them and said, 'With man this is impossible, but not with God; all things are possible with God.'" (Mark 10:27)
- "Come to me, all you who are weary and burdened, and I will give you rest. Take my yoke upon you and learn from me, for I am gentle and humble in heart, and you will find rest for your souls. For my yoke is easy and my burden is light." (Matthew 11:28-30)

Discussion

- Describe a time where you had to trust God.
- Was the result something you needed or wanted?
- Will you still trust God when the outcome is undesirable?

Chapter 7: It Is Only Temporary

"Weeping may endure for a night, but joy comes in the morning"
- Psalms 30:5

The History

In Leviticus 25:23-24, the LORD tells the Israelites that the land should never be sold on a permanent basis. God is the owner of everything, and we are just temporary residents. If land is ever bought or sold, the original owners should be given the opportunity to redeem the land, especially in the Year of Jubilee. We are to revere the Father for who He is by taking care of the land He has given us. This principle would have made the Israelites a stronger community and more appreciative of their blessings. Stewardship is a vital principle in every area of life.

How It Can Apply Today

Today, we think once we buy something that we own it until we decide to sell it again. This can be seen when we buy anything from toys and games to houses and cars. We make our hard-earned money and think that whatever we use it for is ours. God has told us otherwise. He told us that we are only temporary owners of anything under the sun, and we should behave as such. When we begin to treat our "possessions" as God's property, we begin to appreciate them more. Thinking of our things as temporary, we prioritize better. We begin to pay more attention to our relationships with God, family, and friends. We start helping those in need. We start encouraging those who are hurting. We become less consumed by what we have, and more consumed by who we have in our lives.

In the spiritual, Jesus has savED us (yes, I capitalized the -ed on purpose). I heard a message from Pastor Mike Todd of Transformation Church about this subject (Grace Like A Flood series). He talked about how God has saved us in our past, present, and future when we put our faith in Jesus. Sin is only temporary. Many of us, including the body of Christ, hold on to our past mistakes and circumstances because we want to punish ourselves for being less than perfect for God. However, Jesus washed our sins away and made sin temporary in our lives when we yield to the Holy Spirit. We have to acknowledge that sin is temporary so that we can focus on the permanence of God's love and salvation through Jesus. Once we focus on the permanence of God's love, we begin to experience less worry, shame, doubt, fear, and other things that the enemy uses to distract us.

Tips On What You Can Do Now

Here are some beginning steps toward improving our stewardship of everything we are given:

- <u>Set standards for lending and borrowing.</u> Everything we lend and/or borrowed should be valued with a level of care that is greater than how you would treat your own property. Do nothing out of selfish ambition or vain conceit. Rather, in humility value others above yourselves **(Philippians 2:3)**
  - Strive to do your best to manage well what you have borrowed, but extend grace if everything is as good as it was before.

- <u>Remember that we own nuttin'!</u> Keep in mind that everything we have is only temporary and can be taken away. Consistently remind yourself that life is greater than the things we "own" **(Matthew 6:25-34)**
- <u>Hold onto things loosely</u>. Remember how valuable things are, but remember that they are just things at the end of the day. It is okay to own things as long as things don't own you.

Discussion

- How can you re-prioritize permanent and temporary things?
- What can you do to help others now that you have re-prioritized?
- How do you view lending and borrowing now?

Chapter 8: Reclaim Your Family

"If relatives help each other, what evil can hurt them?"
- African Proverb

The History

Leviticus 25:25-28 talks about what the Israelites were to do when one of their own sold the property because of poverty. Since property could not be sold permanently, as we discussed in the previous section, someone could redeem or buy back the property. But since the original owner was too poor to own the land, how could he or she redeem it? Verse 25 tells us that the person's nearest relative could redeem the property for them. That family member would pay the balance of the land and reclaim it for their family. If the original owner later acquired the funds to redeem the land, they could redeem it at any time. If he or she never acquired the proper funds, then the land would be returned in the Year of Jubilee. This principle of family redemption is a way to strengthen the ties that bond the family together.

How It Can Apply Today

The picture at the start of this chapter depicts a man buying the house where he spent his childhood. Today, not many of us would buy back a relative's property after they sold it. If they had fallen on hard times enough to sell their house, how many of us would buy their house back? We might offer to let them stay with us for a while until they get back on their feet, but that's it. We might even give them a little money to help them towards buying another place to live. But none of us would be willing to buy their house back. However, that is exactly what God has commanded us to do. God gave us this principle to show us that we must keep our families tied together through rough times as well as easy times. Next time your brother loses his job and can't afford to pay his bills, pay some of his bills for him. When your sister can't afford to raise her child and is about to put the baby in foster care, help her support the child or even adopt your niece or nephew so that your sister can still be in his/her life. Strengthening family ties brings society together through communication and love while decreasing crime and violence. The family has the power to influence the world, and the breakdown of the family gives control to the enemy. Our families are being destroyed like never before. It is time to redeem our families back to a stronger and brighter future under God.

In the Body of Christ, this concept is our prime directive. **Acts 1:8** tells us that the Holy Spirit will give us the power to be witnesses for Christ in Jerusalem, Judea, Samaria, and to the rest of the world. This means that the body of Christ is to help our fellow brothers and sisters reclaim their spiritual property that they have lost to the enemy or given to others. I used to be a people pleaser. I would do almost anything someone needed even if it wasn't good for me or for them. This caused me to become distant, selfish, and spiritually unavailable to others. God led me through His Word **(Galatians 1)** and sent Christians to help reclaim my spiritual love and desire to help others. If those fellow believers had not helped me along, I'm not sure where I would be in terms of my desire to help and show love to other people. God has commanded us to redeem our family's spiritual property from the hands of the enemy. We must start with our home (Jerusalem) before we try to help the world. Once we fix our home, we can help lead the lost world back to Christ.

Tips On What You Can Do Now

Strong nations are made up of strong communities that are made up of strong churches that are made up of strong families. However, we see that families continue to struggle to stay strong and connected which leads to the breakdown of our churches, communities, and nations. Here are some first steps to helping rebuild and reclaim the strength of our families:

- ASK! This is a very simple way to understand how to help your family heal and grow from any past or present situation.
  - Be careful who you ask and how you ask. Make sure that you are asking someone who has the most correct information as well as someone with a heart and tone of sincerity and no judgment.
- Develop a heart of generosity. Practice giving with a sincere heart. Giving can be financial or service-based. Volunteer time to your local churches or schools; donate to homeless shelters or food banks.
- Forgive any past or present hurts that may be driving a wedge between you and your family.
- Air out dirty laundry. If there are misunderstandings, lies, or even generational curses within your family, seek help to address the root issue(s) and cause(s). Come together with those who want to help the family and formulate a plan on how to address the issues at hand. Reminder: Do so with respect!
  - Seeking professional family counseling is a great option as it will provide a mediator between family members. This process will be difficult, but the resolve to strengthen the family must be stronger than the pain.

Discussion

- What are some hidden/unaddressed issues you and your family need to address?
- Can you act as a mediator during family discussions?
- Are there any estranged relatives to whom you can contact?

Chapter 9: Return The Property

"There is nothing like returning to a place that remains unchanged to find the ways in which you yourself have altered" - Nelson Mandela

The History

Verses 29-34 of Leviticus 25 talk about property within walled cities, property in the open country, and property in the Levitical towns. These three areas were special in the eyes of the Israelites. The walled cities were those which held important property or resources for the people. The walls also served as protection against nations that sought to overtake the city. The most famous walled city in the Old Testament was Jericho. Property sold within walled cities could be redeemed by the seller within a year of selling. If the seller did not redeem after the year was up, the property would remain with the buyer and their families, and not returned in the Year of Jubilee. The property in the towns outside the city walls was considered open land to buy or sell. However, this property was to be returned in the Year of Jubilee. The Bible does not specify why God chose this command for the different types of property. The land owned by the Levites, the people of the clan of Levi, could always be redeemed and returned in the Year of Jubilee. The land given to the Levites were holy places and places of worship for the Israelites. Let's break down how these three different properties relate to us today.

How It Can Apply Today

This topic can be applied to different areas of life from physical housing to mental property and even emotional well-being. I will choose to apply the walled city to our mental property. Mental health is the most important aspect of a person's physical nature. Our minds were made for so many great things, but they can be extremely fragile. God has provided physical walls for our minds (skull) as well as mental walls for our minds (reason, logic, morals). These mental walls protect us against attacks from anything that tries to drag us away from healthy mental living. These things include violence, abuse, neglect, harsh words, discrimination, intimidation, disloyalty, and the like. If we choose to give the well-being of our minds over to these things, the repercussions will change your life and not for the better. Good news: God has given us an allotted period of time for which we must reclaim our property from these things. We can reclaim our mental property through prayer, forgiveness, and counseling. If we do not reclaim our property in the allotted time, then we lose that aspect of our life to someone or something else that does not deserve it. Mental breakdowns of depression, anxiety, substance use disorders, etc all stem from a lack of reclaiming your mental property. Nothing in this world deserves to own our mental health besides us and God. We must be careful what we sell within our walls.

    Open country property can be associated with physical and emotional property. These types of personal property must be returned in the Year of Jubilee. Like we said earlier, because of Jesus Christ, our Year of Jubilee can occur at any time. Returning physical property is easy to do; just give it back to the owner. Emotional property can be a little harder. We grow close to things and/or people in our lives that we cannot let go. We must return the emotional property we own from others and vice versa in the Year of Jubilee. This comes from forgiveness and acceptance that the person or thing does NOT belong to you. Letting go is always the hardest part, but God will provide everything you **need** according to His riches and glory in Christ Jesus (Philippians 4:19, emphasis added).

    The Levitical land represents our spiritual lives. This property has been sold to and stolen by the enemy for far too long. If we sell our spiritual property, i.e. faith, hope, etc., we are giving an important aspect of ourselves to someone who does not have our best interest at heart. However, thank God for Jesus and his finished work on the cross! Thanks to Jesus, we can reclaim our spiritual property at any time because He has broken the chains and released the captive spirits from the hands of the enemy. The moment you choose to reclaim your spiritual property, you must do so in the Name of Jesus Christ! Without Jesus, our spiritual lives would be held hostage by the enemy forever. **John 16:33** NIV states, "I have told you these things, so that in me you may have peace. In this world, you will have trouble. But take heart! I have overcome the world." Reclaiming your spiritual property gives you eternal access to God's grace and mercy.

Tips On What You Can Do Now

Be careful what you allow to be given away in your life. Some things can always be recovered, but some things cannot.

- <u>Know how much value something has</u>, both financially and sentimentally. If something has been in your family for generations or has a special memory attached to it, use wisdom when handling it. Once things are lost, there might not be a chance to get it back. There is a saying that we never know how much something means to us until we don't have it anymore. That sentiment holds true.
- <u>Remember that you can ALWAYS reclaim lost personal values (joy, faith, hope, integrity, truth, and love).</u> These things can only be lost if we give them away to others. You can choose who will receive these things. Determine your self-worth and set standards for the people or situations that will NOT influence these values within yourself.

- <u>Pick your battles</u>. If something is not worth fighting over, do not fight over it. Do not let differing opinions ruin any relationship. Do your best to live in peace with others as long as it does not compromise your character. "If it is possible, as far as it depends on you, live at peace with everyone. Do not take revenge, my dear friends, but leave room for God's wrath, for it is written: "It is mine to avenge; I will repay," says the Lord." **(Romans 12:18-19)**

Discussion

- How can you reclaim personal values?
- How has this chapter changed your perspective on things you value?
- Have you been too careful with personal gifts (tangible and intangible) that need to be used more? Have you been overusing personal gifts that need to be treated more valuably?

Chapter 10: Help The Poor

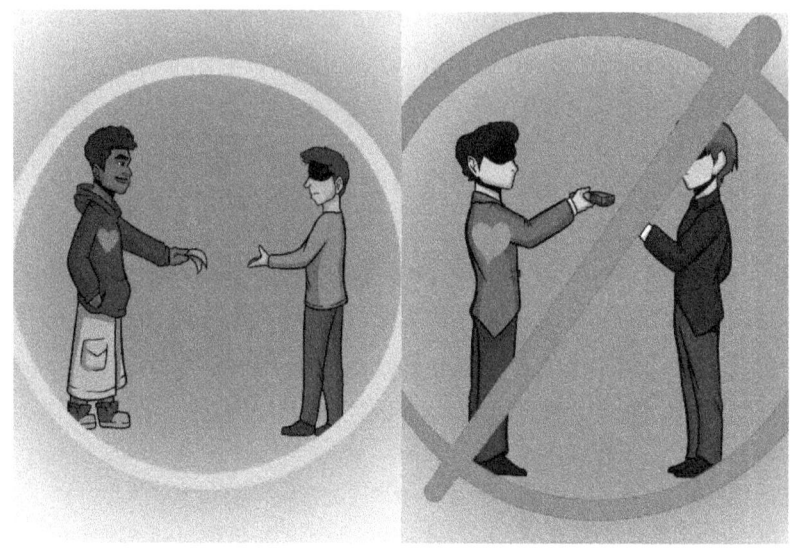

"No one has ever become poor by giving" - Anne Frank

The History

Leviticus 25:35-38 gives instructions on how to treat the poor. We are to help our family, friends, strangers, and foreigners when they need help. If they need food, give it to them without charging to make a profit. If they need money, lend them money without charging interest. They were to follow these instructions out of reverence for God who brought them out of slavery in Egypt. Helping the poor was a huge deal in biblical days. The world was small with many people who did not have all that they needed. God tells his people to care for the poor because He has blessed us so much that we must do the same for others. Today is no different. There are many more people, and with technology, the world is only getting smaller. "Whoever is kind to the poor lends to the Lord, and he will reward them for what they have done." **(Proverbs 19:17 NIV).** Caring for the poor is more important now than it was back then.

How It Can Apply Today

In the United States, and in many areas of the world, we live in a greed-driven society. Everyone is looking out for themselves and occasionally helping the less fortunate (especially during tax season). We are reluctant to give a stranger money on the street because of stereotypes of people using the money for drugs or things other than the intended purpose of the money. In our current political climate, many people dislike foreigners in the United States; those who do speak hate and violence against these innocent people. Many of the foreigners in the U.S. are here because of harsher conditions in their homeland, and they are in search of a better life. But they arrive and experience more hate simply for being themselves. We have a responsibility to help those in need, but not enough of us do our part. These things can influence people not to give. We must give freely from the heart and without expecting anything in return. **2 Corinthians 9:7 NIV** says, "Each of you should give what you have decided in your heart to give, not reluctantly or under compulsion, for God loves a cheerful giver." If God has blessed you with much, you have been given the responsibility to give to others. God requires much from those who have been given plenty (**Luke 12:48**). Once we decide to help the poor without thinking about ourselves, there will be stronger communities, less poverty, improved foreign relations, less ignorance, and the list goes on. We must choose to help these people out of our love for Jesus and take ourselves out of the equation.

    Proverbs 27:17 NIV says, "As iron sharpens iron, so one person sharpens another". In the body of Christ, we must help our poor in spirit. The Kingdom of Heaven belongs to them through Jesus Christ **(Matthew 5)**. When an ironstone sharpens an iron sword, both become stronger, sharper, and ready to perform the task they were created to do. The body of Christ must help those who are growing. We are all on a journey, so those further along must help the new believers as they transition into this walk of faith. Real change only comes when there is someone to hold you accountable. God knew He couldn't save us by Himself, so He put on human flesh as Jesus (God-incarnate) to die for our sins. Jesus knew He couldn't save future generations without a guide to stay behind after He ascended, that's why He gave us the Holy Spirit. God's triune nature makes sure that He does what he set out to do. Search for a spiritual mentor (pastor, Christian friend, counselor, etc.) that will hold you accountable on your journey. We must be willing to grow and help others grow if we are all to exemplify Jesus.

Tips On What You Can Do Now

I chose this title for this section of Leviticus 25 because we ought to have a mindset of helping without expecting anything in return. Helping the poor means to help someone who cannot pay you back.

- Remind yourself not to expect anything in return for helping someone. You will receive a reward in Heaven, but may not always get one on earth. **(Matthew 6:1-4)**
- Treat everyone you meet with the utmost respect. You never know who you could be helping and how it could impact the trajectory of their life. "Do not forget to show hospitality to strangers, for by so doing some people have shown hospitality to angels without knowing it." **(Hebrews 13:2 NIV)**
- Give what you can with an open heart. If you can survive without certain things or a certain amount of money and there's an opportunity to help someone else, GIVE. This may mean giving up some luxury items, such as daily coffee from a coffee shop, entertainment subscriptions, or even convenience. If giving it up could help someone else, consider giving.

Discussion

- List some local community service organizations that have valued that compliment your own.
- How has this chapter changed how to interact with people (family, friends, and strangers)?
- Determine an amount of time, energy, and/or money to give to an organization that helps the poor.

Chapter 11: RELEASE!

"Until we know release, we will never know freedom." - Priscilla Shirer

The History

This is the most important aspect of the Year of Jubilee: release all captives, servants, and debts. Leviticus 25:39-55 explains what the Israelites were to do with their hired servants, slaves, and any debts that were acquired. If Israelites were poor and couldn't afford their livelihood, they could sell themselves as servants to their fellow Israelites. The Israelite servants were to be treated as hired workers instead of slaves, meaning they were paid for their jobs. Since they were Israelites, they were released and returned to their home property in the Year of Jubilee. If the Israelites wanted to buy slaves, they were to do so from the countries around them. The slaves were considered permanent property that could be given to children for life. However, Israelite slaves were treated better than common era slaves. Their slaves were educated, rested on the Sabbath, and joined in traditional worship activities. If a foreigner wanted to buy an Israelite as a slave, their fellow Israelites were to monitor their care to make sure they were not being treated harshly. When it comes to debts, ALL debts were erased during the Year of Jubilee. Servants worked to pay off debts in certain cases, but these debts were canceled permanently in the Year of Jubilee. This sounds like an amazing year for everyone involved. How can we learn from this and improve our lives today?

How It Can Apply Today

Releasing the people of their debts and setting them free is a revolutionary concept in a world filled with greed and pride. Too many people want every dime they feel they are owed from whoever they have helped. This has caused people to feel like they owe others for everything, even gifts. Have you ever said, "How can I return the favor?" when someone gives you a gift or does something for you? The answer is probably yes, I know I have. Today, millions of Americans have student loan debt. These debts were acquired because education is such an important topic for our future. Many aspiring students cannot afford to pay out of pocket for college classes, so they turn to loans to pay for their education. The debt lenders begin to ask for their money back within six months of graduation. This debt thrust upon new graduates, who already struggle to find good-paying jobs, adds another level of stress. If we implemented this concept, the positive ripple effects would be infinite. With forgiven student loan debts, young adults could focus more on their careers, saving money, investing, charitable donations, and spending money in the market. These effects would improve economies, create jobs, and grow businesses, as well as reduce stress levels, reduce depression caused by financial struggles, and improve the overall happiness of life. If these results can occur just from releasing student loan debt, imagine how much more release would happen when considering housing debt, car debt, and national debts.

    This release has even greater results in the spiritual realm. Imagine you're held by chains in your mind and spirit that keep you trapped from progressing, feeling loved, and using the full power given through Jesus Christ as Lord. Many of us do not need to imagine because we live with these chains every day. But now, imagine those chains being released and you being truly free from those negative things holding your spirit hostage. That is the power of the Jubilee. Jesus' death and resurrection set us free from all of this bondage, but many of us put the bondage back on ourselves. But NOW is the time to release yourself from the self-imposed bondage! Now is the time to release yourself and others from the chains that we have created! Set yourself free in the Name of Jesus Christ our Lord! "So if the Son sets you free, you will be free indeed." **(John 8:36 NIV)** You can experience greater joy, love, peace, forgiveness, confidence, self-control, patience, and many more once you release yourself from the bondage! Know the truth of God's love, Jesus' resurrection power, and the Holy Spirit's guiding wisdom. "Then you will know the truth, and the truth will set you free." **(John 8:32 NIV)**

Tips On What You Can Do Now

Release is a powerful tool in any area of life. Releasing tension, pride, hostility, unfruitful people, etc. can work wonders for your own growth and the growth of others.

- Release any lies, half-truths, and secrets that you have been keeping from others, or even yourself. **(John 8: 31-36)** Life is much too short to not be honest with yourself, others, and God.
- Forgive ANY & ALL debts that someone owes you. This release will allow the other person to feel less burden while improving trust between both of you.
- Release the offenders from your past. This is a difficult step, but a necessary one if you are to strengthen your freedom.
    - Seek counseling or other professional help that will be beneficial to your releasing the offender. Remember: forgiveness is not forgetting that the offense happened, but not longer allowing it to dictate your life. What you hold on to has power over you.

- <u>Put Jesus Christ on the throne of your heart.</u> Without Christ, we only have the option of sin (separation from God). If we accept Christ, we now have been given a choice to sin or follow God. True freedom can only be experienced if you have a choice. **(Matthew 6:33, John 15:1-8)**
  - Acknowledge that you have missed the mark of God, turn away from the things that made you miss the mark, and turn to God and allow Him to guide your life since He has your best interests at heart.

Discussion

- Create a list of people you need to forgive, especially if that person is yourself.
- How has this chapter shaped your view of healthy emotional release?
- With whom can you share this information about releasing for overall healthy living?

Conclusion

The Year of Jubilee is a lesser-known command but can have profound results. The Year of Jubilee takes preparation, patience, and most of all faith in God. Trusting God to make all these things happen is going to be tough for our human minds to allow, but once we do, there's no telling how great God will bless us. Obedience to God's Word takes faith in action, reliance upon Jesus, and wisdom from the Holy Spirit. This principle event can have a profound change in our society as we restructure our priorities

The Year of Jubilee is not a consistent way of life. This is a special circumstance that will help create freedom in your life. We should use these principles throughout our lives, not just within the Year of Jubilee. Keep these boundaries on a consistent basis during the non-Jubilee years. Consistency is key when walking with God and within His boundaries. You must wake up each day and make the conscious choice to walk in the steps God has ordered for you. Plan according to your life cycle, including the Year of Jubilee, but walk day by day according to what God says about you and His plans for you.

In the Name of Jesus, I pray that you have gained a new perspective on life. I pray God blesses you, shows you the way to true joy, and causes great things to happen in your future. Amen.

www.ingramcontent.com/pod-product-compliance
Lightning Source LLC
Chambersburg PA
CBHW032217040426
42449CB00005B/648